*I am not a defender of socialism
or big government!*
PAUL KRUGMAN

IN JULY 2015, I debated the Nobel Prize–winning economist Paul Krugman in front of more than 2,000 people at FreedomFest in Las Vegas. This was billed as the economic showdown of the year: the lead economics columnist for the *New York Times* versus the former senior economics writer for the *Wall Street Journal.* The overall theme was "socialism versus capitalism." Do we need more government in the economy to achieve more growth and economic fairness?

The debate was moderated by Mark Skousen, the producer of FreedomFest and presidential fellow at Chapman University. It was cordial, and the back-and-forth was illuminating, especially for understanding the clash of worldview between left and right. But it was primarily a debate about *results*, not ideology. My old boss Representative Dick Armey used to say, "I don't need faith in free markets. I have evidence." Liberalism, alas, is based on wishful thinking and good intentions (but not even always that). I don't think it's any exaggeration to say that Paul Krugman is the most influential left-liberal economist in America today. Democrats and academicians absorb his analyses and recommendations as gospel, so this exchange offers a window into their mindset.

We dueled on almost all the major economic and financial issues in today's national policy discourse and in the presidential campaign – from the minimum wage, to Obamacare, to remedies for our economic malaise. Here I replay highlights of the punches and counterpunches, by quotation and paraphrase, along with some of the supporting graphics that were presented. I have tried to do justice to Krugman's arguments in this abridged version of our debate. At the end of each topic, I have added brief comments in summary. We offered Krugman the opportunity to add his own additional comments, but he declined.

As you will discover, Krugman is witty, well-versed on the issues, and quick on his feet. He is also a staunch advocate of nearly everything that government does — and it's fair to say he thinks that unfettered free-market policies lead to severe inequality and ruinous outcomes. He defended the Postal Service, Obamacare, Medicare, the minimum wage, and the welfare state, which he claims is rapidly shrinking.

I'm biased, but I believe that on nearly all of the issues I carried the day. Krugman knows more about health care than I do, so that discussion may have been a draw. A poll taken of the attendees after the debate showed me the clear winner. Unfortunately, the day before the debate, Krugman vetoed television cameras in the auditorium — no Fox or CNN or C-SPAN. The blackout prevented potentially hundreds of thousands of people from viewing the debate live. Fortunately, a full-length video of the festivities is now available on YouTube. A full transcript is also available on request from *www.freedomfest.com*.

1. *Why did we have a recession, and did the Obama stimulus fail?*

PAUL KRUGMAN

"We just had the mother of all financial crises, or actually the stepmother of all financial crises, because the mother was the 1930s. But this was a pretty close second. And it takes a long time to recover from those even with the best policies, which we did not have." The errors were: "We cut government spending too quickly. We failed to have sufficiently aggressive monetary policies. So it's been a long hangover. Although compared with anyplace else in the advanced world, the U.S. economy looks pretty good right now."

Economic growth has been much slower over the past 30 years than in the three decades following World War II, but "we've done not too badly by many measures." The problem is that the new wealth has not "trickled down to ordinary working families," so we've had rapidly rising inequality in the midst of decent economic growth.

"Just about everything we've done in Washington for the past seven years has been exactly the wrong thing to do. We've made the economy much worse with these governmental interventions. And it's not just under Barack Obama but under George Bush."

The bailouts were a mistake, creating "a great moral hazard for the economy" and bringing about a centralization of the banks. The $830 billion stimulus plan did not create jobs. Obamacare, tax increases, cash for clunkers – all mistakes. The massive spending added $7 trillion to the national debt in six years. It was "a big Keynesian experiment," and did anything go right?

It's true that Obama inherited an economic crisis. But so did Reagan, when we had "20 percent mortgage interest rates and 14 percent inflation, and every economist in the day was saying that America was in permanent decline. And these two presidents used entirely different approaches to dealing with the crisis." Reagan's philosophy in brief: "the government is not the solution, government is the problem." Obama's philosophy: "the government really is the solution to a lot of our problems."

If the Reagan recovery had been replicated under Obama, we would have $2.75 trillion more in GDP and about 5 million more jobs today.

KRUGMAN

"The recessions of 2008–9 and of 1981–82 were very, very different beasts." In the earlier case, "the Federal Reserve wanted to bring down inflation. And it raised interest rates sky high. And then after they felt that the economy had suffered enough, they brought interest rates way down. And so you had a rapid recovery."

In the recent recession, "we'd had a financial system that ran out of control and crashed. And the Fed tried to cut interest rates. But it ran up against the problem that you can't cut interest rates below zero. And that meant that it was a very, very different

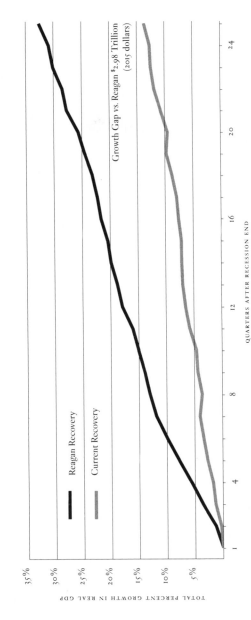

Growth Gap: Current Recovery vs. Reagan Recovery

TOTAL PERCENT GROWTH IN REAL GDP

35%
30%
25%
20%
15%
10%
5%

■ Reagan Recovery

■ Current Recovery

Growth Gap vs. Reagan $2.98 Trillion
(2015 dollars)

1   4   8   12   16   20   24

QUARTERS AFTER RECESSION END

Source: Bureau of Economic Analysis (through Q1 2015)

story. It was bound to be a much slower, a much more difficult recovery, even with the right policies." I kept writing that the recovery was going to be sluggish.

The advanced countries responded to the crisis in various ways: "Some were imposing really harsh austerity, some were not." If you compare "the rate of growth of government spending in any individual country and year with the rate of growth of GDP" in 2010–13, and if you don't "cherry-pick" the data, you'll find "an obvious, strong, positive correlation in recent years between government spending and growth." If spending should have been cut more, how do you explain these numbers? The cross-country data show a "very, very Keynesian" reality.

And the Obama stimulus spending was not gigantic in an economy of $17 trillion a year. "You had an $800 billion stimulus spread over three years. It maxed out at about 2 percent of GDP. It was not a huge program." In fact, "I was tearing my hair out repeatedly on the pages of the *New York Times* saying this is a vastly inadequate stimulus."

As for the challenge to show a successful example of a stimulus plan, the problem is that "nobody ever does it really on the scale that's required when it's needed."

MOORE

"Economists on the left threw the whole Keynesian playbook at this recession, right? Virtually every page of Paul Krugman's book, maybe not to the extent that you wanted it to happen, but it happened. We did spend $850 billion on a stimulus plan. We did borrow $6 to $7 trillion over six years. And the return on investment was terrible."

Would we be better off if we had borrowed $10 trillion and added another $3 trillion to the debt? "We would probably be Greece."

In the past, Paul wrote that the deeper the recession, the stronger the recovery. "And that's actually exactly what happened under Reagan. We saw the stock market fall by two-thirds in real terms in the decade before Reagan. That was a financial crisis par excellence, and Reagan came in and it wasn't just the Fed policies that changed." There was "the big reduction in tax rates, the supply-side recovery, the deregulation of key industries, the getting government at least partially under control, and a pro-business atmosphere. And those policies did create one of the most powerful recoveries."

But the Obama policies failed to meet the administration's own projections. "The Obama people in 2008 told us what would happen if we had an $850 billion stimulus and what would happen if we didn't have the stimulus." As it turned out, "we actually had higher unemployment with the stimulus than the Obama people said we would have if we had done nothing."

KRUGMAN

"This was a foolish forecast. And notice they were predicting that it would be a short-lived

Unemployment Rate With and Without Recovery Plan

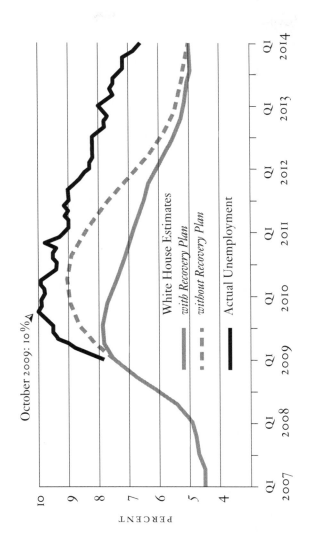

PERCENT

October 2009: 10%

White House Estimates
with Recovery Plan
without Recovery Plan

Actual Unemployment

Q1 2007   Q1 2008   Q1 2009   Q1 2010   Q1 2011   Q1 2012   Q1 2013   Q1 2014

recession, that we'd recover quickly even without the plan. However, it's not what I predicted. They just didn't want to be as pessimistic as history said they should be. The aftermath of a financial crisis is always a slow recovery."

Citing the Reagan recovery is "pretty weak evidence." Here are five presidents "in order of growth rate of the economy under their watch: Clinton, Reagan, Obama, Bush I, Bush II." Now, explain "why Clinton, who began with a large tax increase at the top, actually had a slightly better growth rate during his period in office than Reagan," and "why George W. Bush, who did substantial tax cuts, did not preside over a successful economy."

Actually, the Clinton tax hike was "largely irrelevant" to the 1990s boom. The point is: "There are only certain times where you really need government intervention. The 1990s was not one of them, but post-2008 it really was."

I did overestimate the negative impact of the Clinton tax increase, but most of what Clinton did on the economy was pretty good. In essence, it was "an anti-Keynesian stimulus, because the government as a share of GDP fell substantially under Bill Clinton's presidency," from about 23 percent of GDP at the beginning, to around 19 percent at the end. "It contradicts just what you said, that government spending stimulates the economy."

Additional Comments

Krugman was one of the most important voices on the left calling for massive government spending and borrowing to rescue the economy in 2008. So essentially we got the "Krugman stimulus." And it didn't work.

He maintained that the 2008 financial crisis was so catastrophic that 2 percent growth was the best we could expect. He resorted to the familiar argument that financial crises take longer to recover from – up to 10 years.

Yet when the economy boomed in the 1980s, he argued that it was a natural snapback and that the deeper the recession, the stronger the recovery. So which is it?

When I brought up the Reagan recovery for comparison, Krugman huffed, "Is this the best you've got?" But the Obama recovery is well behind *all six* other post-1960 recoveries, and Krugman's explanation is that the stimulus was way too small relative to GDP and could have been twice as big. This is a common argument of the left: when their policies fail, they fall back on counterfactuals that are impossible to refute. We will never know what would have happened if the government had borrowed $10 to $14 trillion instead of a little over $7 trillion, but the idea that it would have fixed the economy seems implausible, to say the least.

Krugman presented a chart indicating that countries employing Keynesian spending grew faster than those applying austerity measures. But the chart covered just three years of data, 2010–13. (Talk about cherry-picking data!) Dr. Salim Furth, my colleague at the Heritage Foundation, pointed out in February 2014 that "Greece was the apotheosis of Keynesian stimulus – spending for spending's sake, lax tax collection, and a government committed to borrowing at the low prevailing interest rates. And Greece was not the exception; it was just the extreme. The next largest deficits were in Ireland, Spain, and Portugal, which had miserable growth. The Eurozone experience since 2007 does little to commend Keynesianism." The lesson is "more taxes means less growth," although the relationship between diminished government spending and a decline in economic output is "less clear."

Krugman and the Keynesians talk about "austerity," but fail to distinguish between the economic ramifications of tax increases vs. government spending cuts. As Alberto Alesina and Veronique de Rugy noted in a Heritage analysis, "In the pursuit of austerity, the important question has less to do with the size of the austerity package than with the type of austerity measures that are implemented." In the debate, I observed that the impact of government spending on GDP growth in 2009–12 was neutral at best. Big-spending nations didn't come out of the recession any more powerfully than those that didn't open the floodgates. Germany refrained from big spending initiatives and fared much better than most of Europe. But what really had a negative impact on growth was tax increases. Nations that cut taxes in response to the recession did better than the ones that raised taxes. In other words, the outcome of fiscal policy variables was a supply-side, not a demand-side phenomenon.

2. *Will Obamacare eventually lead to socialized medicine or a single-payer system? And would that be a good thing?*

KRUGMAN

"I don't think we will have socialized medicine." Obamacare is a hybrid, with "regulation and subsidies to sort of channel the private sector into covering the bulk of the population. And it's working actually quite well."

We already have a "single-payer system called Medicare that covers Americans over 65. And it is extremely popular. It could be cheaper," although "as best we can tell, it's cheaper than private insurance. It works."

Moreover, "Every other advanced country has some form of universal coverage." While Britain's government-run system "has its problems, as every system does, it's enormously popular." The system in the United States, with Medicare and now Obamacare, "seems to be working reasonably well." We will probably continue "to use private insurance companies as the principal mechanism to deliver health insurance."

And Obamacare "has been coming in way cheaper than expected." The cost of providing insurance coverage has been about 20 percent below the Congressional Budget Office's prediction. There's been a "glitch" in sign-up numbers because many states rejected the Medicaid expansion, but in those that

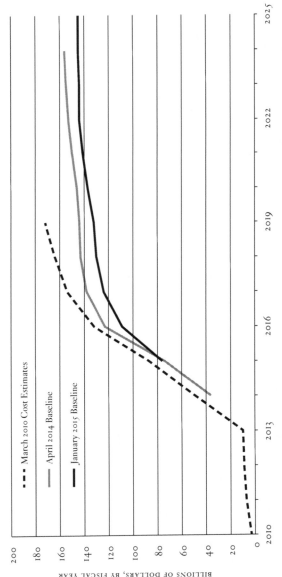

Comparison of CBO and JCT's Estimates of the Net Budgetary Effects of the Coverage Provisions of the Affordable Care Act

Sources: Congressional Budget Office; staff of the Joint Committee on Taxation

Note: These numbers exclude effects on the deficit of provisions of the Affordable Care Act that are not related to insurance coverage and effects on discretionary spending

accepted it "we're about three-quarters of the way towards the intended amount of insurance coverage."

The CBO looked into "what would happen to the U.S. budget if we repealed Obamacare." Answer: the deficit would increase. So Obamacare is coming in below budget through a combination of tax increases and cost-saving measures. "This is a remarkable success of public policy."

MOORE

"Let's look at the big picture of government interference in health care." In the American economy, "there have been two sectors over the last 30 years where prices have risen spectacularly out of control." Those sectors are education and health care, arguably the industries most dominated by government.

Adding more government control to health care has never driven down costs. "Every time we've seen an expansion of government health care – whether it's Medicaid, Medicare, S-Chip, all these programs – they lead to an

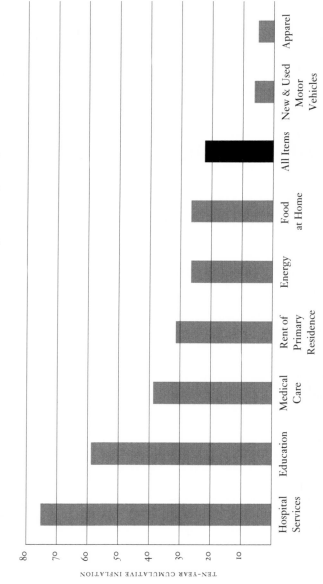

Ten-Year Inflation, Ending in May 2015

increase in the inflation rate in health care. And it's the same thing with education. When you have a third party paying for these things, it drives up cost."

With Obamacare, "something like 15 to 20 states have already advertised what the increases in premiums will be next year. You're looking at about 10, 15, 20, in some cases 25 to 50 percent increases in premiums. How is that a good deal for the American patient? I thought this was a program that was gonna save $2,500 per patient."

Then there's the medical device tax, a "preposterously stupid" idea, "because the future of health care is innovation. We want more drugs. We want more vaccines. We want more lifesaving devices. Would you agree with me, Paul, that when you tax something you get less of it? So why in the world would we want to put a tax on medical devices?"

KRUGMAN

"You have actually just explained why health care costs rise," but inflation in health care is not out of control. "The biggest reason health care costs rise is that medical innovation keeps on delivering new things we can do." In the past, if you had heart problems, the doctor "would possibly give you some aspirin, basically suggest that the family spend a lot of time with you because you didn't have much time left. Now you get a triple coronary bypass. And we want that." The problem is that "we haven't done a very good job of figuring out when to stop."

If government intervention is the problem, why does every other advanced country have much lower health care costs? Switzerland has the most privatized system among them, and it's also closest to the United States in terms of cost. In all the others, costs are 50 or 60 percent of ours.

As for "horror stories about the quality of health care in other countries, it's not true. It varies." But "French health care, with about 60 percent of our cost, is superb. British health care, with about 40 percent of our cost, is not so superb." Overall, the results aren't much different from ours. "So if there was any place where it really looks like government does a more efficient job than the private sector, it's health care."

It's true that "where someone else pays the bill, then there's going to be incentive issues. The doctor wants to do as much treatment as possible. The patient wants as much treatment as possible." That's a problem "whether it's a private insurance company or the government is paying the bills."

In any case, "when you get sick it is very, very expensive. And nobody except multimillionaires can afford to do without insurance. So it's a question of making insurance work. And one of the ways you make that work is by creating incentives so the excessive spending on procedures of dubious medical benefit is somewhat limited."

MOORE

"You're wrong on this issue of insurance not being a driver of the cost." Remember that "some procedures are 100 percent covered by insurance, and others are not. Yes, it is true that rapid innovation is driving these higher costs. As we become a richer society, people want to spend more on health care."

But look at Lasik surgery, which is not covered by insurance. "There's no third-party-payment problem with that. And what has happened to the cost of Lasik surgery? It's fallen because people have to pay out of pocket. In fact, they advertise on TV: 'I'll do it for less than this guy does it.' You don't have that with other types of procedures because either the government or the insurance programs are paying for it."

KRUGMAN

"It's an optional procedure," and besides, "I know a number of people for whom Obamacare has been an enormous literal lifesaver. . . . I know people who never had health insurance. I know people who needed to change jobs and the new job didn't come with health insurance and they got breast cancer. There are millions of stories like that out there." Moore's world might just be too narrow to include such people.

"I know some people are paying more. We knew that was going to happen. But overwhelmingly, the effects have been positive and in many cases just enormous personal gains."

MOORE

The Republicans ought to repeal Obamacare, as they have vowed. But we don't necessarily need to repeal it. Just give every American a voucher, $7,000 or $8,000, so they can "buy whatever kind of health insurance they want. Let people have a thousand choices." People on the left talk about "freedom to choose," so why must everyone have the same health care plan?

People should have "stylized individual choices" in health insurance because we don't all have the same risk tolerance and so on. A voucher plan would drive down costs. The Republican position should be: "Go out and buy whatever insurance you want."

Krugman says that nowhere has government been more successful than in health care. He favors a single-payer system and argues that socialist systems provide as good or better health outcomes at lower cost around the world. Medicare is apparently the glittering success story of government, yet it is running unfunded liabilities in the tens of trillions of dollars. There is no denying that a third-party-payer system is driving up costs in health care and education.

Krugman claims that health savings accounts and other consumer-oriented plans can't work because no one is going to shop around for a doctor during a heart attack. But in the Internet age, people do shop around for treatment of many conditions and learn about alternatives and costs. People who get cancer or need other specialized care can become experts on the Web. Patient-directed care works.

The more highly a service is covered by third-party insurance, the faster the rate of inflation for that service. If Obamacare is such a victory, why are health care premiums rising much faster than Obama predicted? Where is the $2,500 per family in savings?

3. *Do you think it is a good idea to raise the minimum wage?*

KRUGMAN

"This is someplace where I have actually changed my views. And I've done it for a rather peculiar reason, because there was actually evidence that came in....

"I used to believe the conventional wisdom 25 years ago, even among liberals. Even liberal economists used to believe that raising the minimum wage was likely to increase structural unemployment. That's still surely true at high enough levels."

But we have something like controlled experiments where one state increases its minimum wage while a neighboring state does not. Likewise with neighboring counties. Looking at these situations, "you just cannot find evidence that raising the minimum wage from the levels which now prevail in the United States costs jobs." The reason is "probably that labor markets are a lot less perfectly competitive than we think, that there's a lot of market power on the part of the employers, that there are offsetting issues, like slightly higher wage increases for retention of workers." Pooling many different studies on these natural experiments shows that "the effect of the minimum wage on employment is zero," or nearly zero.

"So I'm for minimum wages up to somewhat higher levels than we now have. If you asked $15, I'm good; $20, I would say, 'Let's wait and see what $15 does.'" Early indications from Seattle don't show the adverse effects that people warned about. But give it another year or two.

MOORE

"Back in 2013 you wrote in your textbook that there are displacement effects from raising the minimum wage."

"That's Econ 101. And most of the time, Econ 101 is right, but there's overwhelming evidence now that in this case it turns out not to be."

MOORE

"Where I see a big impact is actually on teenagers. There's a mythology that there's all these people who are heads of households who are working at the minimum wage," and it's nonsense. "The vast majority of people who are on the minimum wage are below the age of 29. About half of them are teenagers. And most of them are in the fast-food restaurant or the retail industry."

A lot of research shows that raising the minimum wage reduces labor force participation for teenagers. Our economy now is hurting from a drop in the labor force participation rate, which has fallen particularly among people under the age of 30.

"This is a very sinister trend because if people don't start working till they're 19 or 20

Employment-to-Population Ratio, Ages 16–19

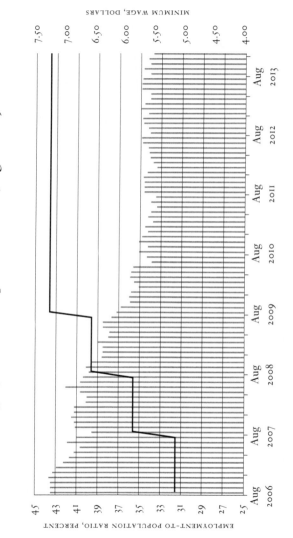

Sources: Bureau of Labor Statistics

or 22 or 24 – that's the Europe model – they never catch up in terms of wages and productivity. There's a lot of good evidence that if you start working at 15 or 16 or 17 years old, that pays dividends down the road when you're 30 or 40 or 50 years old."

With only 4 or 5 percent of Americans working at minimum wage, "we spend way too much time sweating on this." But what about a teen minimum wage of, say, $5 or $6 an hour? "I have two teenage sons.... I would do anything for them," except "I would never pay them $12 an hour because they're not worth it. So what do you do for someone who's not worth $10 or $12? Are you saying they can't work?"

KRUGMAN

"The evidence just doesn't support that," so "let's go outside and duel with our econometrics studies." Anyway, "my gut instinct on a teen wage is that policy shouldn't be too complicated – that you probably shouldn't do it. But I'm willing to think about it."

Krugman argued for a minimum wage of $15 an hour, and if that works, go to $20. When I cited his own textbook admitting that raising the minimum wage has displacement effects, he said that he had changed his mind based on evidence. But the evidence has not changed. We have seen a negative effect of the minimum wage in declining labor force participation among young people. A teen minimum wage would be a no-brainer.

4. *Are "red states" growing faster than "blue states," and if so, why?*

MOORE

"The biggest economic and demographic trend in America is this 'red state / blue state' divide. I'm not saying red states are Republican, 'rah, rah, rah,' and blue states are Democrat and bad. But you get states that are red that are moving more toward free-market policies. And blue states are, to put it simply, adopting the policies that Paul Krugman endorses."

Today, "you're seeing about 1,000 people a day moving from blue states to red states." Blue states are losing workers, business, capital, and families; they are declining in importance. "The economic center of gravity in America is moving southward," or, more specifically, to "the states that have the right sets of policies."

The biggest states are Texas, Florida, California, and New York. "One out of every three Americans lives in those four states. So it matters a lot what happens there." They divide into two sets that are quite different in their economic policies.

"What is the income tax rate in Texas and Florida? Zero. What is the highest income tax rate now in California and New York City? It's 13.3 percent. California and New York are not right-to-work states. They're forced union states. Texas and Florida are right-to-work states." And those are explanations for where jobs go. "Texas and Florida allow drilling. California and New York don't allow drilling. Texas and Florida have light regulations. California and New York have a lot of regulations, and have outlawed fracking."

Over the last 15 years (or any period in the past 50 years), "for every job that has been created in New York and California, there have been three jobs created in Texas and Florida. California over the last 10 years has lost 1.5 million people. Florida and Texas on net have gained them. California's making a comeback right now. But their long-term trend is very negative."

KRUGMAN

The picture for job growth over the last year is just the opposite, with "pretty fast growth in a bunch of blue states, some red states as well, very poor in the middle of the country."

The question is: "What causes what? When you see directional change, causation is always the problem. And sometimes the causation is reversed. Sometimes there's a third factor that determines both politics and economic performance."

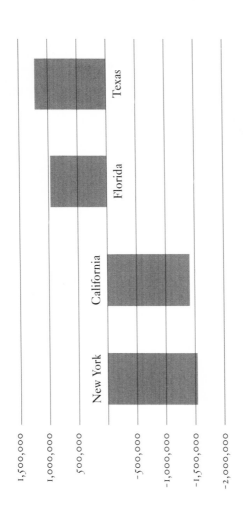

Domestic Net Migration, 2004–2013

For example, in January 2011, Sam Brownback became governor of Kansas and Jerry Brown became governor of California. ("I feel decades younger all of a sudden!") California took a left turn; Kansas turned right. And the employment data show California doing much better than Kansas since then.

"That's as close as you're gonna get to a controlled experiment in the effects of economic policies on state levels of growth. And while Texas is continuing to do really well and is a big powerhouse for jobs, certainly the 'Kansas experiment,' as Sam Brownback calls it, has not succeeded." Meanwhile, the "dire predictions" about the tax increase and the left turn in California didn't come true.

As for longer-term growth rates, "I actually turn a lot to Ed Glazer, who happens to be a Republican." According to Glazer and others, the exogenous factor that correlates most strongly with faster growth is warm winters. "That's overwhelmingly the case. Places that have warm winters have grown

Employment Growth: Texas, California, Kansas

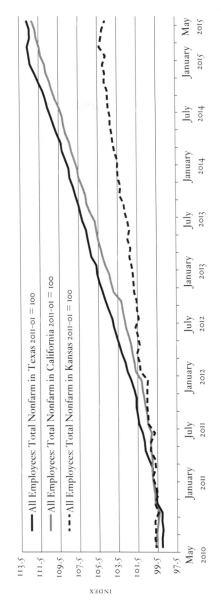

— All Employees: Total Nonfarm in Texas 2011-01 = 100
— All Employees: Total Nonfarm in California 2011-01 = 100
--- All Employees: Total Nonfarm in Kansas 2011-01 = 100

INDEX

113.5
111.5
109.5
107.5
105.5
103.5
101.5
99.5
97.5

May 2010
January 2011
July 2011
January 2012
July 2012
January 2013
July 2013
January 2014
July 2014
January 2015
May 2015

faster." If you ask why people didn't always move there, the answer is air conditioning.

MOORE

"Really? Your answer to this is air conditioning? Wow."

KRUGMAN

"It's an amazingly slow process. It was not that long ago that Houston was considered an impossible place to live – actually, I think it still is. Anyway that's a whole 'nother story." Back to the point: "it used to be that U.S. population was concentrated either in places that were settled very early or in places that were near the great coalfields of the Appalachians." Over time there's been "a slow, slow adjustment to warmer winters."

In terms of policy, red states are substantially better than blue states when it comes to land use. "The Northeast and the West Coast are both the lands of Nimbyism." (*Not in my back yard.*) They have "extremely restrictive land-use policies. California is a crowded state now, as is New York, as is New Jersey. But the housing prices don't have to be nearly as high as they are. And it's the restrictive land-use policies, the zoning, that makes it very hard."

Texas does very well, and "if you actually ask what really motivates people to move to Texas, not many people are moving there for the taxes. They're moving there for the cheap housing."

There could be many factors, but "the things that seem to be the best explanations of differential state growth are weather and land-use policies." It just happens that "conservative states tend to be warm states. And that has deep roots in American history which we probably don't want to get into." Those states "tend to be growing faster. But the idea that it's all about income taxes is just not borne out by any independent studies."

MOORE

"You cannot explain people moving from San

Diego to Houston because of the weather. It's almost preposterous."

KRUGMAN

"I meet people all the time who are saying, you know, 'I can actually afford a house if I move to Texas.' That's a much bigger factor."

MOORE

"You're right. Almost everything costs less in Texas than in New York or California, no question about it. The cost of services, the cost of educating a kid, the cost of paving a mile of highway – everything is cheaper.... But that's not exogenous. Those are the policies that have been put in place: the environmental regulations, the labor regulations, the taxes. All of those things get embedded in making things cheaper in Texas."

KRUGMAN

"It's overwhelmingly just land-use policies. If you go down the road in Texas, for a Northeasterner, it's pretty striking. People can build pretty much whatever they want wherever they want. You can have an adult bookstore next to a church. I'm for it."

Additional Comments

Of all the issues we butted heads on, Krugman was least persuasive in explaining the red state / blue state phenomenon and the mass migration of nearly 1,000 people a day from blue to red America. Blue states follow Krugman's advice with higher tax rates, costly welfare programs, forced union laws, and tort systems that reward trial lawyers over people and businesses.

Faced with the far superior economic performance of Texas and Florida over California and New York, Krugman trotted out Kansas, where taxes were cut and the economy didn't boom. He ignored what has happened in states like Connecticut and Illinois where tax hikes have had catastrophic consequences and have failed to balance budgets while sending jobs southward. He argues that California, with its high taxes and heavy regulation, is flourishing. But over the course of a decade, 2004–13, California lost nearly 1.5 million residents to other states. And California has some of the most severe inequality in the nation. This is a success?

5. Why are so many socialistic nations like Greece failing?

MOORE

"What's going on in the world right now is an incredible repudiation of socialism. And all of these places that have turned to socialism – Greece, Puerto Rico, Connecticut, Detroit – are going bankrupt."

KRUGMAN

"I'm not a socialist but I'm an advocate of a strong social safety net. People on the right in the U.S. are for small government. People on the left are not for big government as a goal in itself. They may favor some policies that would make government bigger, some that would make it smaller." And I'm really "not a big-government guy. I just don't think that government is always the problem. Sometimes government is the solution. Reagan was wrong."

MOORE

"Government has done a terrible job when it's done things like try to run the steel industry or the post office."

KRUGMAN

"No, the post office operates under some political constraints. But those are there for a reason. And government actually does pretty well at running health care, it turns out. The evidence is pretty overwhelming there. But anyway, it's not a doctrinaire thing on my part. It's a point of view of how things actually seem to work."

Additional Comments

My main argument against Krugman was that socialism, progressivism, Krugmanism – whatever *ism* you want to call it – is collapsing everywhere. From Argentina to Greece to Euroland writ large. These socialistic states have high tax rates, generous welfare benefits, strong unions, a tight regulatory environment, and all the other things Krugman preaches. As a result, Greece is now functionally bankrupt.

Krugman argued that the creditors are being too harsh and that the Greek government has imposed too much austerity; but while the private economy shrinks, the government's role remains far too large. Despite some reductions in actual government spending since 2009, the rate of spending in proportion to GDP soared: from under 45 percent in 2005, to 59 percent in 2013, and still 49 percent in 2014. The debt as a share of GDP has soared to more than 175 percent. Over the past decade, there has been a spending splurge, not austerity.

What Greece needs is a big supply-side tax cut (a flat tax), privatization of just about all government assets, and deregulation of industry to get the private sector growing.

You don't do that by growing the government and public debt.

6. *If you had a choice among the big three in economics – those would be Adam Smith representing perhaps laissez faire; John Maynard Keynes, who favored some form of big government, it seems; or Karl Marx – which would you consider the greatest economist?*

KRUGMAN

"As my old teacher Paul Samuelson said, people are always complaining that Marx is being misinterpreted. But after 50 people have had an accident at the same intersection, you stop blaming the drivers." That leaves Adam Smith and John Maynard Keynes as my two great economists.

Adam Smith was "not at all the extreme free-market guy that I think many people in this room imagine." In fact, he was "very much for strong bank regulation," because "the first modern banking crisis had taken place in Scotland a few years before he wrote

The Wealth of Nations." Smith had a metaphor: "Saying that it's a restriction on liberty to regulate banks tightly is like saying it's a restriction on liberty to require that people put up firewalls in adjoining houses." Some things are necessary in the public interest.

"So Adam Smith was not pure laissez faire. He understood the power of markets. He also understood their limitations, which I'm afraid is something that a lot of people have lost in this country."

Keynes, for his part, "explained how it was possible for economies to go so badly off the rails." Read his essay on "The Great Depression of 1930," change a few words and archaic phrases, and it's "a wonderfully accurate description of what has happened to the world economy in recent years."

MOORE

"There was a great article in the *Journal of Economic Literature* five or six years ago, called 'The Age of Milton Friedman.'" According to this article, "the period between the early

1980s and around 2005 was the greatest period of wealth creation in the history of civilization," when "about a billion people, or one out of six or seven on the globe, moved out of dire poverty and moved out of starvation and malnutrition."

In the span of history, 25 years is the blink of an eye, and "during that period you had one of the great economic miracles of all time." China moved more toward capitalism, privatizing much of its economy. Likewise India.

By contrast, "the last decade has been the age of John Maynard Keynes. And it hasn't worked very well. Every time we try to put in place all of these Keynesian macroeconomic policies, they fail. They failed in the United States. They failed in Europe. They failed in Greece. They failed in Argentina. I mean, when, where have they ever worked? They didn't work in the 1930s, for goodness' sake! The Great Depression was a result of government intervention."

7. *Do you favor welfare reform?*

KRUGMAN

"I dispute the premise that welfare spending is out of control. It just ain't so. Just look at spending on income-related transfers. Look at income support programs in the federal budget. There is no upward trend in those programs as a share of GDP until the Great Recession hits." It's a myth that more people are living on government support in times of prosperity.

"Then we have the worst economic slump since the 1930s. Surprise, a lot of people turn to safety net programs," and those programs "made a very, very big difference." We didn't see people selling apples on the street. We didn't have shantytowns. We had a social safety net that "alleviated some of the worst misery. In fact, these last seven years have been a triumph for the American welfare state because we got through a period of catastrophic financial crisis" while "extreme human suffering was substantially limited."

Today, welfare rolls are shrinking; food stamp spending is falling; and "unemployment benefits have dropped back to traditional levels as a share of the economy." Many Americans who receive government benefits deny it. Medicare recipients will say they're not beneficiaries of any government program. But we really don't have "a large number of people who are opting out of the economy, choosing not to work because of these general social programs."

MOORE

"I am in favor of a social safety net. We're the richest country in the world. We can afford to make sure that people don't go hungry at night. We can make sure that people have health insurance and so on."

But consider what happened in 1996, when Bill Clinton signed a welfare reform bill that changed the rules, basically saying: "You've got a two-year time limit and then you're off. If you have an additional child while you're already on welfare, we're not going to pay you additional benefits. And most importantly, we're going to require you to be looking for work or get a job."

It's true that the economy was improving greatly during that time, and it's also true that the number of people on welfare dropped by an unprecedented measure. The statistics show that "a lot of the welfare recipients, especially welfare mothers, moved into the workforce," and many saw their incomes go up.

"If you look at poverty in America today, the people in the bottom 20 percent, over half of those households have no one working. You can't climb the economic ladder if no one's working." So why not have work requirements in the welfare programs?

KRUGMAN

"I'm not as hardline against the welfare reform as you might think. The old welfare system was dysfunctional. It was a system that, among other things, was designed only for mothers. And that was mothers without a male presence. And that was a bad system."

Today, however, "we have no system for providing income. We have systems for providing supplements in the form of food stamps. We have unemployment benefits if you were working." But if we periodically have a sustained economic slump, we need a stronger safety net.

This issue is "fairly trivial," however, since we've already reformed welfare. "AFDC is no more. Instead, food stamps and Medicaid have become the core of our welfare state. And they are both good programs" that "do a lot to alleviate suffering. They're both run quite efficiently. They're okay."

MOORE

"Well, there's a third big one, and that's unemployment insurance.... I don't know if you're familiar with the North Carolina experiment, but back in 2012 they dramatically reduced the size of the unemployment insurance benefit. And they also substantially reduced the number of weeks you can get benefits. And what happened was that the unemployment rate in North Carolina fell more than in any other state. It was a very successful program."

KRUGMAN

"It was largely a labor force participation issue because people no longer felt that they had to say they were looking for work anyway, and that is why the unemployment rate dropped."

MOORE

"But they had a huge increase in jobs too. It worked in North Carolina. It can work all over the country."

8. *What three things would you do to fix the American economy?*

KRUGMAN

"I'm gonna start with a really big one: the land-use issue. It's not just that it makes housing expensive." In addition, "because of the way the regulation is distributed, the restrictions on land use are actually pushing people away from the states where worker productivity is the highest into states where it's lower." For example, "output per worker is lower in Texas than it is in the Northeast. But people move there largely because it's too expensive to buy a house in the Northeast."

Second would be "something like universal pre-K support. One of the great tragedies of America right now is how much human potential is lost because we are a highly unequal society, and children who make the mistake of choosing the wrong parents just do not in fact get an even break." Consequently, "rich, dumb kids are more likely to graduate from college than poor, smart kids. We need to do everything we can to help children," and that's the next project – assuming that health care is working.

Third is "a general program of trying to empower workers again, starting with minimum wage.... We used to have a very strong private-sector labor movement" along with "a lot of policies that enhanced the bargaining power of workers. We had those policies during the 30 years after World War II, which were the period of most rapid, most successful economic growth in the history of America. And it was widely shared growth," so that "everybody's living standard doubled."

Then, "in 1980, we began dismantling all of that. And since 1980 we've had growth that's not too bad on the whole," although "it's not as fast as it was during the postwar generation." Worse, the growth has been "enormously concentrated in the hands of a relatively small minority at the top."

One remedy would be to "increase the bargaining power of workers. Make it easier, once again, for them to organize. Raise minimum wages." The concept is "pre-distribution," not becoming like Cuba. In moderation, these policies can lead to more widely spread prosperity in a growing economy.

MOORE

"I want a widely shared prosperity as well. I think it's the most important thing. The question we should be asking in this upcoming election and for the next 10 years is 'What do we do to help the middle class?' Everything that has been done for the last six or seven years has actually reduced the status of the middle class."

As for unions, they "contaminate everything they touch. The steel industry and the auto industry and the state and local governments." Unions are "a bankrupting institution."

Yes, we need to help families in the lower 20 to 25 percent. Many of them are broken families – more than half with no father in the household. Marriage is a great economic institution, and yet "we actually discourage people from getting married under the welfare laws."

The first reform would be to "give a voucher of $8,000, $10,000, $12,000 – you choose the number. And let every single child in America, whether they're rich or poor, have the same kinds of options that Barack Obama had with his two daughters."

Second reform: private Social Security accounts. If Paul is correct that the greater returns in our economy go to capital, "then why in the world shouldn't we make every worker in America capitalist? Let them own the company they work for and put 8 to 10 percent of their paycheck into private accounts so they can own a piece of the rock." Today, Social Security is probably the worst financial deal a young person will ever make, with a return of close to zero percent. "Private accounts would give workers a much better return."

Third, "let's blow up the tax system and have a simple 16 or 17 percent tax rate. Everybody pays the same rate. Get rid of all the complexity. Get rid of all the loopholes that the rich take advantage of. And I actually think if you do that, the rich will pay a higher share of the tax burden. But you're going to have explosive growth. We'd see what happened in Texas all over this country."

KRUGMAN

"Or maybe what happened in Kansas all over this country."

Social Security vs. the Market
Real rates of return

- Social Security average income

    Two-earner couple   0.78%

    Single worker   0.31%

- U.S. stock market, 1802–2001   6.90%

- Large-cap stocks, 1926–2013   8.90%

- Small-cap stocks, 1926–2013   13.20%

- Portfolio: 60% stocks/40% bonds, 1926–2013   5.50%

Sources: Cato Institute, Jeremy Siegel, Ibbotson Association, National Bureau of Economic Research

---

MOORE

"Kansas had more job growth than Illinois and most other blue states."

Kudos to Paul Krugman for going into enemy territory and debating economics. I had the home-field advantage, but the audience treated Krugman with respect and an open mind. That's more than I can say when I speak to liberal crowds.

I'm sure most readers will agree that he was not very persuasive. He blamed Republicans, George W. Bush, Art Laffer, Steve Moore, and "tax cuts and deregulation" for the Great Recession. I couldn't resist poking fun at him for never taking responsibility for his own policy blunders. In August 2002 he advised: "To fight this recession the Fed needs more than a snapback; it needs soaring household spending to offset moribund business investment. And to do that … Alan Greenspan needs to create a housing bubble to replace the Nasdaq bubble."

We got the Krugman housing bubble, and the rest is history.

My big takeaway from the debate is that advocates of free-market capitalism need to call out the Krugman, Obama, *New York Times*, Hillary Clinton, IMF crowd for being so wrong in so many places around the world with their wildly irresponsible debt and spending policies. Free markets didn't cause Greece or Detroit or Puerto Rico to fail. Supporters of statism are rightfully on the run because, in states and cities and nations around the globe, their model is imploding right before our eyes.

If we look around the world or across the United States, we can see that the left's obsession with income inequality and wealth redistribution is only making the poor poorer and driving the middle class downward. Much of the world is in another economic crisis now and poverty is rising again, while middle-class voters are in a state of revolt. Krugman's model has failed.

No wonder he didn't want the debate to be televised.

© 2016 by Stephen Moore

First American edition published in 2016 by Encounter Books,
an activity of Encounter for Culture and Education, Inc.,
a nonprofit, tax exempt corporation.
Encounter Books website address: www.encounterbooks.com

Manufactured in the United States and printed on
acid-free paper. The paper used in this publication meets
the minimum requirements of ANSI/NISO z39.48–1992
(R 1997) (*Permanence of Paper*).

FIRST AMERICAN EDITION

LIBRARY OF CONGRESS
CATALOGING-IN-PUBLICATION DATA
IS AVAILABLE

10 9 8 7 6 5 4 3 2 1